Art Of Life

A COLLECTION OF ORIGINAL QUOTES
AND MUSINGS

Written by Damon Lee Patterson

I0473623

ISBN: 978-0-615-86929-2

Book design by Damon Lee Patterson

www.artsavedmylife.com

Printed in the United States of America

First Edition

There is a single frequency that cuts through all space and time. It is the beginning, the middle, and the end. All other frequencies are connected to this single-source vibration. It is the root note of the universe. You can feel it. You get glimpses. It flirts with you in different forms within your dreams. Clues of its existence are scattered around the world in ancient art and spiritual text. You are made from it. It's always present, perpetually ringing out. The only way to explain it is to describe love, bliss, wholeness, peace, fulfillment, creativity, and inspiration. It is the thread that bonds us. It is my hope that these collections bring you closer to this frequency and allow you to uncover it in your everyday life. This is a collection of my most potent thoughts and epiphanies. These words have been compiled from my notebooks, digital recorders, emails to myself, my social media profiles, scrap paper, and my dreams. I present to you "Art of Life.".

Art Of Life

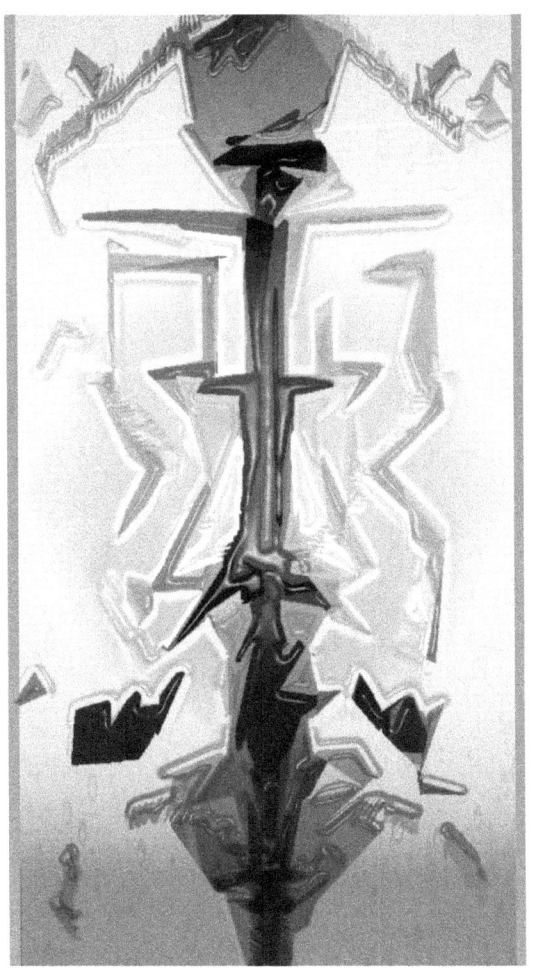

SPIRITUALITY

We are eternal beings visiting earth in human bodies/spaceships.

ONCE you digest who your true father/mother is...you will know without a shadow of doubt royal blood travels through your veins (kings queens princes princesses young gods and goddesses)

Mother Earth is in a relationship with Father Spirit and we are their offspring.

Embrace your higher self.

At times I imagine everyone was in a spiritual realm without bodies staring at Planet Earth asking to be a part of it. Like oooh god that place looks magical and beautiful...I want to go there! (Like an excited kid) Then he says ok.... Ill send you there and Ill embed magical gifts within you to help you navigate. Some of these gifts are instantly accessible. Some unlocked at specific times. So here we are on Planet Earth that magical place we looked upon long ago with our magical abilities. We only have to remember.

It all started when one wondered what it would be like to be two.

Maybe the stars in the sky look up at us and think the same thoughts that we think of them.

Learn to look at everything as if it were a mirror...cause everything is absorbing and reflecting something.

It is difficult to see something that is all around you.

The creator does NOT make mistakes. Humans just have a limited point of view and a limited amount of understanding.

In our pursuit for abundance we are as silly as a fish in the ocean looking for water.

It's difficult to see your purpose because you are living it everyday.

If you experience heaven leave yourself and others clues!

The universe is like ONE big orchestra or music box playing a never-ending song.

Planet Earth is boot camp or school for spiritual beings.

Every thought is a prayer.

This isn't new. You've always been here.
This isn't home I'm just passing through.

We all need to practice mental levitation and spend more time with our higher self.

We will all have our time out in the wilderness with nothing but faith.

The dark forces are busy...the good must be just as busy...even more.

There's common denominators within all religions and spiritual teachings. Its the principle of the one yet many or the source of all things and the infinite now.

Everything is present right now. Yesterday tomorrow and forever is all happening now.

Listen to what god is telling YOU. Surely he's not done with divine inspiration.

Faith is ->believing<- that the creator knows what's best for you and the confidence that he/she will deliver as promised even when YOU don't see how it is possible.

Darkness playing like light. I know who you are. You can't hide. You always leave dirty traces of your self. You always speak the same way. You always act the same way. No matter whose face you steal!

Thank the creator for beauty and being able to perceive it!

The creator always catches me right before I hit the ground and when he lets me hit rock bottom there is always something valuable to see. "Damon don't panic" is what I have to remind myself every time...Keep your eyes open...he's trying to show you something down there.

Don't worry about proving your value to people. Someone will always misunderstand your intention and color it with their on perception. Just know that god has been there with you every step of the way and he/she knows and understands you and everything you wish people did.

If you don't know what you believe in people will tell you what you should believe in.

Faith is priceless.

Life is training wheels, mirrors, and reminders.

A higher intelligence behind all this is the only thing that makes sense to me.

I believe god is in everything, everyone, and everywhere and at all times.

I have no unique message...and I don't want one...I only hope to be in harmony with the message the whole universe has been speaking all along.

Today the creator woke me up as the sun was rising and reminded that I was alive. I thought I was alone...but the heat from the sunrays touched my skin, air filled my lungs, and told

me I was foolish to think such a thing. We are never alone. Everything we need is always near.

Have you ever been in the presence of a force sooooo great and marvelous it made you feel unworthy to be in its grace? (Tears of joy)

Perhaps your life's story is a book in the bible being read by people in the future.

I love when people call to talk to me about how god is moving in their life!

The creator of the universe is the greatest artist of all!!!

Only god knows a persons whole story. He knows why we are, how we are, and how we got to where we are. We are not fit to judge. We truly can only see from our perspective, everything else is a guess.

Give it up! It's not a robbery when god takes from us. He/she is the original owner of everything. We are just borrowers.

You ever think about the fact that we are not our bodies...we are something else (spirit/energy) driving the body? This is just a uniform we must wear while here.

This world is NOT all there is to life! There is more!

The timing of the creator is amazing. Follow your intuition...that's how god guides us.

The older I get the less I want to be in anything. I don't want to be in a car, a house, clothing, shoes, or a body.

If the entire world is all walking in one direction and GOD tells you to walk another way...don't worry about what the masses are doing. YOU walk the other way!

At the end of my day when I am no longer in this body. I hope the creator is happy with how I lived the life given to me. That is all.

Inspired means "in spirit" so creating is spiritual by nature.

Reminder: God uses people to share blessings. The loving light of the creator shines through people. We are those people. Be that every chance you get.

You do you and don't worry about the rest.... some peoples purpose is to try and bring you down.... haters will always be just that.... just make sure your not that. The negative spirit will ALWAYS have something negative to say about everything. It's NOT the person. It's the entity driving their body and they don't even know it!

Don't give up on your dreams. It may sometime look like nothing is happening but trust me JUST KEEP GOING! From our limited point of

view we cant always see what god is doing but just KEEP GOING!

Leave judgment and revenge to the creator...he is the only one who can do it fair with a balanced view...he's the one that wrote the story!

You're pregnant with your eternal self.

Angels are here. They walk amongst us. You are one of them.

Divine intervention happens all the time.

Blessings are not always in disguise.

We are here because we are supposed to be here.

You have to get out and participate with life then it will participate with you.

Don't limit god to your books, leaders, and buildings. There is no place he/she is not. All land is sacred ground.

We are children of the creator of the universe. Now lets act like it. Make mom/dad proud!

I'm not arrogant for thinking I am a powerful being or thinking that the creator is always with me...I'm arrogant if I think I'm the only one.

We must first see and recognize the blessing we have already been given.

Explore what god gives you. Explore what is shown to you.

Hold on be patient. Have faith.... trust the work being done in YOU. If he/she can handle creating the universe...he/she can handle what's happening in your life.

Some spirits were bothering me the other day...they kept playing with my electronics turning stuff off and on while I was trying to work. I nicely explained that they didn't have to do what they were doing. I told them that unlike them I was limited in my human body and they were free to roam the vast universe unhindered then I told them to tell everyone else the same thing...then they left me alone!

Anyone who teaches that the creator of the universe is here and not there or over there and not here etc is teaching you wrong and under the influence of something that is not in your best interest.

Omnipresent means present in all places at all times. Omnipotent means unlimited power or universal power. Omniscient means all knowing. The teaching should align with those principles. The only reason anyone would teach exclusivity in the name is to make profits from the congregation point blank. It's never been about physical places or people. That's what many of these wars are being carried out about. The spirit

is everywhere, in the known, and unknown universe and the spirit is infinite.

I believe the creator works through, in, and with every-ones life. There is nothing more beautiful, magical, inspiring, uplifting, and humbling than being aware of it as its happening...watch him/her/it work in your life...its amazing to witness!

Happy joyful at peace to know that "the spirit" cant be shaken or moved. No matter what type of mental programming or physical harm tried. It is UNTOUCHABLE! You can kill the physical person but the principles of "the spirit" in them is eternal

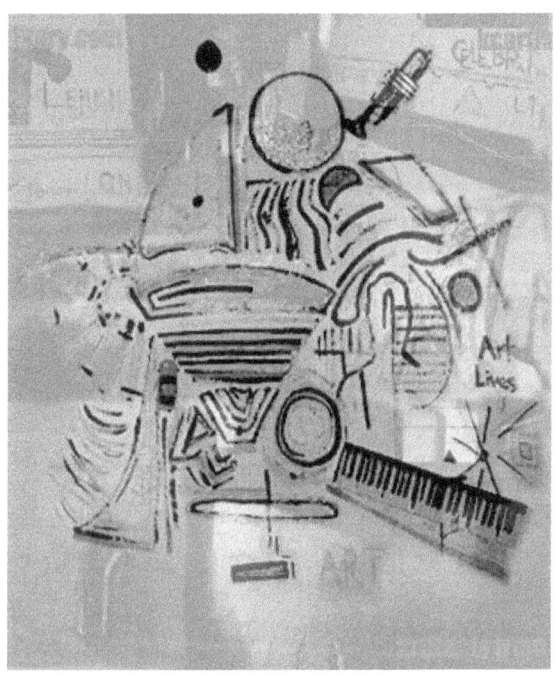

CREATIVITY

Beautiful art is what we think and feel when we are speechless.

Everyone has a magic wand. Use it wisely.

Inspiration is a clue/hint. Listen to it.

The healing arts are indeed ART forms. Maybe the most important, overlooked, under rated art forms of them all!

Finding inspiration externally is wonderful and necessary at times...but to learn to inspire ones self from within will give your stride through life perpetual motion!

Create a vision and then physically grow into it.

Careful what words you put after "I" and "I am"

Use your gifts. We are all the missing piece.

Artists have to be activists. All that creative power is not just for making money and getting fame. It can be used to improve the human condition and the environment. The greatest artists knew/know this.

The universe is full of space and abundant energy. Speak your dreams into existence. Work while you wait.

We create tomorrow today.

Prepare to stand and fight alone...there will be "times" where YOU will be the only one that can see your vision.

If you see something the world is missing...chances are...YOU are the one that should create it.

Art is a road map that the driver can continuously expand on and draw new roads to travel and in doing so we expand ourselves and where we may ___ travel.

Every time I get inspired I have a creative baby.

It is crucial that you learn to inspire yourself.

I didn't really experience life until I started nurturing my gifts. That's when all the invisible doors started opening and the magical people appeared so that's the drum I'm beating until it doesn't work anymore.

One of the greatest moments is when someone who inspires you tells you that you inspire him or her.

You better believe what your projecting and manifesting. The universe is not a game. What you ask for WILL show up and shock you if you don't take your self serious.

One action can change your whole life.

I define art as anything manifested in the physical realm from the act of focusing energy and attention on a vision.

Use the current tools the BEST you can and the universe will grant you access to better ones.

I am moved by what else we can create.

In an interview Michael Jackson was asked what advice he had for up and coming artist. MJ said know more about your craft than anyone alive, hard work, and practice EVERYDAY! If you look at his body of work that attitude reflects.

The best ideas are not forced at all. They kind of just happen or unfold in your head.

I believe in magic because I've been blessed to create it and witness it. Be still and you will become aware of the magic that is all around you at every moment.

God gave each of us gifts. Some are innate abilities programmed in our DNA. Some must be nurtured and developed more than others but they are all there within you.

Create what's missing.

What if...is very powerful for an artist. If is like a key to the imagination. Seeing "it" is a major part of making it real.

Some artists use their gifts to change the mood of a room...some go further and use their gifts to change the mood of a city...a rare select few will go even further and change the mood of the world.

Work toward making your dreams come true even when you are not inspired.

It is up to no one but YOU to make YOUR dreams come true. Only YOU. No one can see what YOU see anyway.

It starts as a thought...then it shows up in physical form.

Love is a lot like water. It can shift its shape and fit in any form or situation. If your trying to make something chances are mixing a little love with it will make __ it happen.

Encourage and support the dreams of those around you...we are all connected in some way.

Create what you seek.

The best way to stay inspired is to keep doing what you love.

The best way to thank god for your gifts and blessings is by using & sharing them.

We have to be participants in other people's dreams also.

Use your art to heal, uplift, and energize community.

One day the woman I create and make reference to in my art will show up to dance with me in real life. (she did)

Don't be afraid to make a fool of yourself.

I think some artists don't do so well in relationships because they are use to getting EXACTLY want they want and need out of their art immediately in proportion to the energy and thought they put in and it just doesn't work that way with people + its hard balancing giving your all to something and still having something left for a person.

If you're a singer..sing! If you're a writer..write! If you're a dancer...dance! If you're a musician..make music! If you're a carpenter..build! If you seek peace...be peaceful! If you seek love...LOVE! If you seek change..change! The right time is ALWAYS NOW!

DO NOT let not having money get in the way of creating and going after your dreams...just start...work together and DO THE WORK!

The first person that has to believe in your dreams is YOU.... if you don't...don't expect others to believe in you.

Amazing beautiful things happen when you just let go and allow it to happen.

I love creating because its one of the only things that truly keeps me engaged and no matter how much I learn or grow there's always more skills/techniques to learn. I struggle with a particular task then once I get it I can put it behind me and start discovering the next thing I need to know how to do. It's endless!

Something really magical happens when gifted people work together.

Your dreams CAN come true. It's all up to you.

Once I succeed with my dreams I'm going to make sure I reach back and help others do the same.

At some point I want to live everywhere. Basically travel to every possible place on the planet and work with phenomenal artists from all over the world.

The ability to walk into a space with one thing then come out with something else is my greatest fascination with creativity.

I absolutely LOVE LOVE LOVE seeing people go after their dreams!!!!!

If we put just as much energy into the solution(s) as we do the problem we could change the whole world for the better tomorrow.

All people are artist. There is an "art" to everything. All activities in life apply some form of creativity.

Don't ever be afraid to express yourself.

I just need to create...that is what I was created to do.

Whenever one of my dreams come true I am moved to help others make their dreams come true!

If I wasn't an artist I'm sure someone would try and lock me up and put me on mind meds...I see shit....I hear voices talking and singing.... and I hear sounds.... sometimes I bust out laughing cause I see jokes in my head...and I know for a fact there is always more than the eye can see going on around us!

You can always tell which songwriters have REALLY been in love or have love in their heart.

Insomnia and creativity are good friends.

Learn the history of your craft.

The only way I can say some things is through my art.

Arrogance is over clocked confidence. Why would the audience feel the need to applaud if the performers clap for themselves ON STAGE? Patting ones self on the back often leaves no room for the audience to do so. Let your art speak for itself.

Art Saved My Life is a literal statement. If it comes off sensational, its because it is. Art has been my sword and shield.

Some projects take moments to be fully revealed to you others may take years...don't force it.

Dreams do come true. Just keep at it and remember hard work is what gets it done.

Dreams need action.

Even if you are not pursuing as a career...art is very healthy to have in your life as a hobby...its good to have something to channel all of lifes crazy experiences into.

Wishing and dreaming is great for having a vision but after it's all said and done it will be the hard work that made it happen.

If you're a rapper and you want to make songs that are timeless you have to write about subjects that are timeless...THE HUMAN CONDITION.... for   example William

Shakespeare has been in rotation since the
1500s because he wrote about subjects that
will ALWAYS be relevant.

It feels like time ceases to exist when you're
doing what you love. It's like moving in hyper
speed and standing still simultaneous ly

Where there is no door CREATE ONE!

My heart is sooo full of love for life and my
mind is always full of ideas.... it only makes
sense that I was born to create...because it will
not leave me alone day or night resting or
awake and creative environments is the only
place I feel fully welcomed and appreciated.

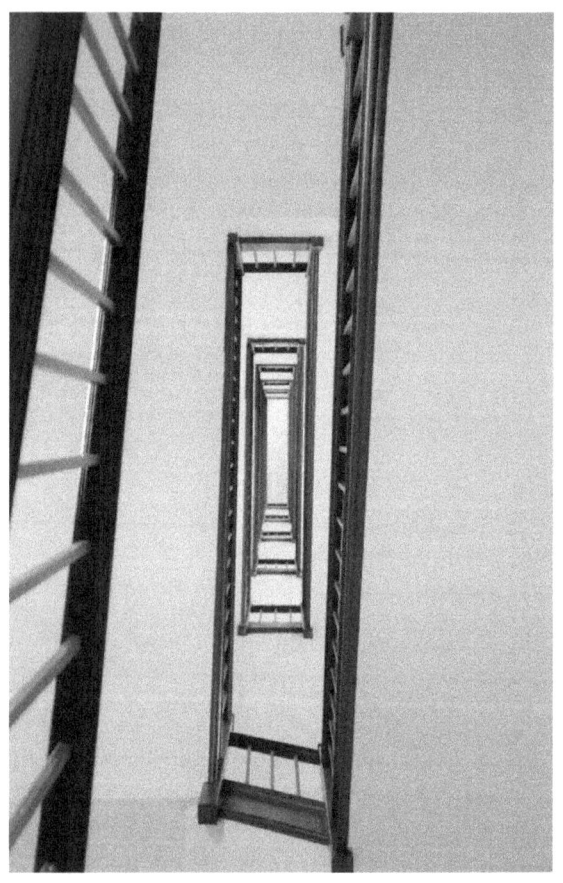

Art Of Life

SUCCESS

In our pursuit for abundance we are as silly as a fish in the ocean looking for water.

Just STAY on course and YOU WILL get there.

It happens when your ready so get ready and it will happen!

Always talk to the boss. Get to the bottom of it. Go to the source or person. Start at the root.

Whatever career you choose become it. Study the greats, study failure, and success. Know more about it than anyone alive, all the ends and outs past and present. Then you have the right to carry the torch into the future.

Blessings are given to those who bless others.

If you act like you can do it all by yourself and need no ones help...don't be surprised when people let you.

Sometimes you have to get all the way off track to see the tracks again. again...

Be flexible. It's true change is constant.

What's even more shocking than none of your dreams coming true is all of them coming true.

Learn to swim before the boat trip.

Nothing is better than having peace within. Id rather live a simple quiet life at peace with my existence than be rich and in torment.

What is possible is all up to what you believe is possible.

If you are waiting on a sign to show up...you may be waiting forever. Action(s) gets it done. Just start where you are, with who you are, with what you have, and give it all you got. If giving your dreams all you have is too much you don't really want it and you don't deserve it.

Each project leads me to the next one. There's always clues to where I should go next within where I've already been.

Prepare your self to receive what you ask for. You are going to get it. Don't worry about when or how...just make sure you are in a position to handle it when it comes.

To ask for abundance is redundant. We live in it. We are made of it. You only have to acknowledge it and express gratitude.

"I can't" is one of the most dangerous phrases. When you use it you shut down the possibilities.

Repeat after me...."My struggle is my fuel" Once you own it...you will lift off!

Take advice from your future self. The you that has achieved all you dream of.

Truly try. Take a step. Give it a shot the best you can and god will start filling in what's missing.

Dwelling on yesterdays rain can make you miss out on today's sunshine if you let it.

It's a new day. Let it be so.

The people who have taken their lives to great heights and experience success had to first THINK and BELIEVE they could or else they would have never even tried.

Only a fool stomps and yells near sleeping crocodiles when he or she could just quietly walk by them.

Just ASK and prepare yourself to receive by being grateful for what is already there.

What you are aiming to be is already within you.

Life knocks you down because it enjoys seeing you get up.

Your time is your most valuable asset.

The time and energy you spend whining, bickering, complaining, and focusing on what's wrong (with self & others) is time and energy that could be used to be productive.

Pay attention to the cues that life gives you. They let you know what you should do next. Let go of fear and ride the wave. There is nothing to be afraid of.

You must master your current level first before you can move to the next.

Being able to turn down a million dollar deal and still being able to sleep at night because the deal went against your moral code. That's integrity.

Don't let YOU stop YOU from moving forward!

First declare it. Then do the work to back up what you declare.

When the turbulence hits, hold the wheel tighter with both hands keep focused on the road ahead.

We must get to the point that our belief in ourselves is as sure as our belief in others.

Sometime you have to take a step first and then the stone/ground will appear beneath your feet.

Your greatest moments will not be planned.

You only fail when you give up.

Don't be unprepared when the opportunity knocks. It WILL keep moving. Visualize your GREATEST level of success.... then prepare for that moment. Use what you already have then build out from there. (Reverse engineer)

It's never too soon or too late to start making your dreams real. If anyone is contemplating reaching for something...just start wherever you are. If you are waiting on the right time or circumstance that time may never come. Just

go for it! The more you put into it the more it really counts and adds up. Dreams REALLY do come true everyday!

Figure out how not to spend money.

Keep going through the wiggles, the detours, the pit stops, the over, the under, around, the loops, and etc..... it's all necessary!

There WILL come a point when faith is all you have.

Others doubting you isn't and shouldn't be your concern. You doubting you is a much bigger issue.

How far you take it is really up to how much you can handle and that's up to you as well.

It's much easier to find someone that knows and admits that they are lost. Pretenders don't send signals and will not receive help.

If you go through hell and get out make sure nothing is following you!

Life can drastically change in the blink of an eye.

You should dedicate at least one hr. a day to reading & studying your craft. Learn more earn more.

One sure way of not achieving your dreams is giving into laziness.

It doesn't matter who you know or how well off they are. You still have to put work in to get where you're going.

Blessings are all around us. Be grateful for the ones you can see and more will start to show.

We attract what we put out and only you have control of what that is.

If you're not where you want to be don't give up. Keep going. Don't be discouraged. You

are meant to be there. In every moment there is something to learn. Use the time to make sure you're fully prepared for when you are where you want to be.

No matter how difficult the journey is at times. There is no greater feeling than waking up and living in the dream that you envisioned for yourself in the past. My advice to anyone pursuing his or her dreams is to JUST KEEP GOING, give it all you got, and remain a student no matter how much you learn. There is always room to grow and get better at what you do. Focus on the work at hand. Everything else will fall in place. Any wall will come down if you just keep pounding on it hard and long enough.

It's not easy changing your whole lifestyle but it's a must if you want to grow and reach your full potential.

Never give up. Things change.

There's no such thing as coincidence or luck. Life follows a divine plan. Every step is fulfilling your destiny.

If you truly believe in your heart that what you're reaching for is your purpose...don't give up no matter what....you never know how close you are!

Get over yourself and make "it" happen.

You're blessed if you have people in you're life that truly look out for your best interest but really its up to you to make sure you're on the right track.

Whatever you're reaching for.... whatever your dreams are.... you may not be where you see yourself yet but just make sure you stay prepared at all times in every situation because you don't know when or how the chance will present itself to you.

No one gets there without some kind of help from somebody. Be thankful for those that help you and be thankful if you helped someone get to where they were going.

NO ONE can defeat YOU like YOU can.

The amount of time and energy invested into something cannot be faked.

At some point you have to get tired of almost and leap.

When carbon is put under 7000 metric tons of pressure it can create a diamond. Gold must be put in fire about 2000 degrees to refine it. Iron must be heated to about 400 degrees and hammered in order to bend it and take on new shapes. A space shuttle burns about 1,607,185 pounds of fuel to leave earth's atmosphere. As people I think we must go through similar circumstance to SHINE bright, achieve our greatest dreams, and reveal/refine our inner gifts & treasures.

We could all wake up tomorrow and decide to do things a different way.

There is no such thing as too deep...too positive...too happy...too smart...too uplifting.

Too hopeful...too philosophical...too optimistic…trying to be too good...too thoughtful...too caring...too giving.... THE DEVIL IS A LIE!

Manage your inner voice. Think bigger. Work harder. Stay out of your comfort zone. Growth happens outside your usual thought patterns and settings. You will only go as far as you expect yourself to go.

Cancel envy and jealousy out of your life. The universe is abundant. There is more than enough for everyone.

Break your own record every chance you get.

If you doubt your SELF how do you expect anyone else to have confidence in you?

When you lose something….something better is on the way. Doors close and new doors are revealed soon after...just don't give up.

Tune your self to your path, dreams, and goals...stay in close proximity to what you're reaching for...be/do that at all times...

Just keep going (consistency) and do your
BEST (Quality) no matter what.
(Determination) Behave and THINK as if you

are already where and WHO you need to
BE!!!!! (Manifestation & Affirmation) Before
you know it you will look back and see that
you are living your dream.

Keep going especially when it's difficult.

There will always be distractions in some
form. Stay true to your plan, your dream, your
goal, your heart, your intuition.

It's a wonderful feeling when you're working
on a project and you get that feeling that what
you're doing is exactly what you're suppose to
be doing.

People will dislike you, not agree with you,
talk bad about you, hate you, misunderstand
you, put words in your mouth, misjudge your
actions etc..... no matter what you do...so its
best to just continue on your path in life and

just do the best you can...you alone will never satisfy ALL humans.

Difficult does not mean impossible. Impossible means beyond ones current level

of perception or know how. We must always remember much of what we see in today's world was at one time thought to be impossible.

Know yourself. Stay focused. Don't let all these distractions take you under. Do what you have to do. Get it done!

Money is just a byproduct. People don't become wealthy cause they chased and caught money....they become successful because they worked hard and made themselves valuable. By creating a quality "wanted" or "needed" product or service. Then money comes to them.

Keep your machete handy when you get off the beaten path.

Sometimes you have to "lose it" in order to "find it"

If you can't find a job create one.

First you have to give it all you got then something else happens that hasn't happen before. It's near the edge of your limits where the growth and magic lives.

Perspective really is everything. Stop damning and cursing your path/life. YOUR ears and eyes are the first to see and hear the negativity you put out to others. You are setting yourself up for failure when you own the negative outlook. If you think positive your life will reflect that attitude. Life is moving forward at all times with or without us. Life is a grand progression. Get in tune with YOUR positive vision.

You are as great as you desire to be and how much work you're willing to do to make your vision real.

Break through whatever is in your way.

It's crucial to speak and have counsel with elders in your arena.

Know what you, your time, and energy are worth.

You can if you think you can.

Having a team that trusts your vision(s) & decisions is crucial. You must have a team to make big moves and be in more than one place at once.

You have to believe it's possible first. Then you will have the courage to do it.

Take a detour if you need but get back on track.

Continue your work with or without the help you think you need.

It's all about how you respond to life. Life can really throw some crazy sh*t at you but you always have options as far as how you respond to it. Keep an open mind. When it looks like there's no way it may just mean you need to open your mind up a little more.

IF you work hard at it...the energy WILL BE transferred!

While trying to make it to the "next level" you must use what is around you/with you/available on the current level...you must get through the current level to get to the next. If you feel u r missing something. Just look around you...its there!

Once the problem is revealed its best to spend time and energy on the solution.

If you are asked to do something chances are it means you can.

Walk toward your destination until the bus arrives.

A major part of being successful and great and what you do is appreciating and respecting the beauty and success of others.

The greatest feeling in the world is watching what was once in your head (dreams) come to life (reality) it's insane!

Some things require that you give it all you got. When you think you've given all you can remember you have more. You are a champion.

There is no such thing as dreaming too big are setting expectations too high.

Your name will make it there before you do.

If you spend your time worried and focused on other peoples flaws.... you will never have time to work on your flaws.

Sometimes we have to reintroduce our self to our old friends. Don't let yesterdays you fool you into thinking you cant be the you of tomorrow.

Greatness lurks.... an eternal tease.... a perpetual glimpse forever flashing in the hallways of thy mind...pushing pulling lifting...edging us on...asking us to meet the challenge.

LOVE

Love can appear to be many things because everything in existence is tied to it...Love is

the source for everything that is was and will be...and it doesn't need humans to believe or practice it to exist.

Do what you love...follow your bliss and what you're looking for will find you.

Its a big mistake to try and force someone to love you...force is always a no no.

A little loving goes a long way.

Love already won.

There's no off button when you love what you do. "It" is ever present where ever you are whatever you're doing.

When negativity comes to you stand your ground and be mindful of the reflection you give. Do the opposite and always remember the way of love.

Love all the hate away & tell fear no.

Remember love when hate shows its face.

Align your self with what you love and the rest falls in place...focus on the work.

You can only hold as much of a river that fits in your hands but never the whole river and even that much you must let go. I'm starting to think of love the same way.

The most important thing for children to see is love.

People who love are brave.

Not expressing how much you love someone is just as bad as pretending you love someone more than you really   do.

I'm totally convinced that the message the universe/the creator is trying to get across to life/us is unconditional LOVE. That's why those who can truly love unconditionally are the most attractive!

You will be treated badly but I implore you to love anyway.

Love is winning.

Someone is in love with you. Maybe you know maybe you don't but someone is all the way in love with you.

Turn up the volume on love. Can we do that?

Don't let them fool you. Love doesn't leave you confused, sad, stressed, tired, drained, insecure, and controlled. It's all the way the opposite. Forget all those silly words spoken. How does it feel when it's all said and done?

Sometimes you know exactly why you love someone. Sometimes you don't…you just know that you do.

The worst fraud artists are the ones that pretend they love you.

People can feel when you love them. I thinking saying it is just confirmation.

Love all the pain away.

I'm happy people still believe in love.

I was born romantic. I'm in love with love because its love.

You can't force a person to love you but you can show them that you do.

Use all your love up while you're here. Don't waste any holding back.

Love somebody.

Love somebody.... none of this other stuff matters!

People who care are ___ brave.

Love endlessly unconditional.

Love is what keeps us.

We live forever but not in these bodies. Don't wait until people no longer occupy them to show how much you love them. Show it everyday as much as possible. Go do it now and don't stop!

Love is the highest form of intelligence.

Life is a whole different world when you spend your time doing what you love.

Love somebody all the time. Its what makes this whole thing work.

The world is full of enough discouraging stuff. Say something uplifting. Say something to make someone's day better. Be an inspiration. Just cause you're unhappy doesn't mean you have to spread that. LOVE MORE.

As long as I can still love Ill be fine.

Tell your loved ones you love them every chance you get.

Love more! It feels way greater than hate!

Love full time.

Do for your loved ones what u want them to do for you.

You know you REALLY love someone when you run out of ways to express it and you enjoy trying to come up with new ways to express how much you love them.

Most of the time people have no idea how much you love them. Even if you've expressed it to them before you still have to remind them again.

Through it all continue to love.

The light is always green when it comes to choosing to love.

Your love can shield your loved ones.

Love wins...love is the all time undisputed champion.

Belief and love are the most powerful forces on earth.

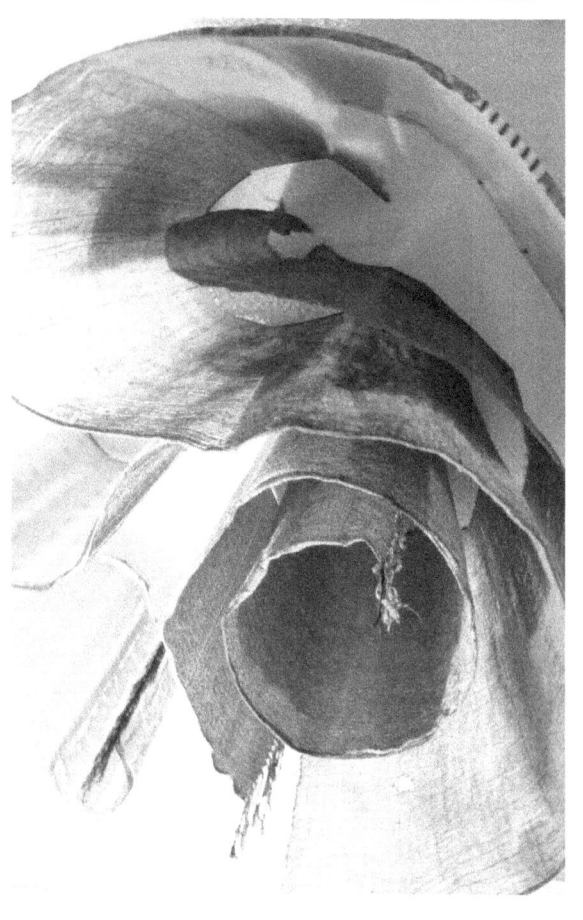

LOVE

Love can appear to be many things because everything in existence is tied to it...Love is the source for everything that is was and will be...and it doesn't need humans to believe or practice it to exist.

Do what you love...follow your bliss and what you're looking for will find you.

Its a big mistake to try and force someone to love you...force is always a no no.

A little loving goes a long way.

Love already won.

There's no off button when you love what you do. "It" is ever present where ever you are whatever you're doing.

When negativity comes to you stand your ground and be mindful of the reflection you give. Do the opposite and always remember the way of love.

Love all the hate away & tell fear no.

Remember love when hate shows its face.

Align your self with what you love and the rest falls in place...focus on the work.

You can only hold as much of a river that fits in your hands but never the whole river and even that much you must let go. I'm starting to think of love the same way.

The most important thing for children to see is love.

People who love are brave.

Not expressing how much you love someone is just as bad as pretending you love someone more than you really do.

I'm totally convinced that the message the universe/the creator is trying to get across to life/us is unconditional LOVE. That's why those who can truly love unconditionally are the most attractive!

You will be treated badly but I implore you to love anyway.

Love is winning.

Someone is in love with you. Maybe you know maybe you don't but someone is all the way in love with you.

Turn up the volume on love. Can we do that?

Don't let them fool you. Love doesn't leave you confused, sad, stressed, tired, drained, insecure, and controlled. It's all the way the opposite. Forget all those silly words spoken. How does it feel when it's all said and done?

Sometimes you know exactly why you love someone. Sometimes you don't…you just know that you do.

The worst fraud artists are the ones that pretend they love you.

People can feel when you love them. I thinking saying it is just confirmation.

Love all the pain away.

I'm happy people still believe in love.

I was born romantic. I'm in love with love because its love.

You can't force a person to love you but you can show them that you do.

Use all your love up while you're here. Don't waste any holding back.

Love somebody.

Love somebody.... none of this other stuff matters!

People who care are brave.

Love endlessly unconditional.

Love is what keeps us.

We live forever but not in these bodies. Don't wait until people no longer occupy them to show how much you love them. Show it everyday as much as possible. Go do it now and don't stop!

Love is the highest form of intelligence.

Life is a whole different world when you spend your time doing what you love.

Love somebody all the time. Its what makes this whole thing work.

The world is full of enough discouraging stuff. Say something uplifting. Say something to make someone's day better. Be an inspiration. Just cause you're unhappy doesn't mean you have to spread that. LOVE MORE.

As long as I can still love Ill be fine.

Tell your loved ones you love them every chance you get.

Love more! It feels way greater than hate!

Love full time.

Do for your loved ones what u want them to do for you.

You know you REALLY love someone when you run out of ways to express it and you enjoy trying to come up with new ways to express how much you love them.

Most of the time people have no idea how much you love them. Even if you've expressed it to them before you still have to remind them again.

Through it all continue to love.

The light is always green when it comes to choosing to love.

Your love can shield your loved ones.

Love wins...love is the all time undisputed champion.

Belief and love are the most powerful forces on earth.

Art Of Life

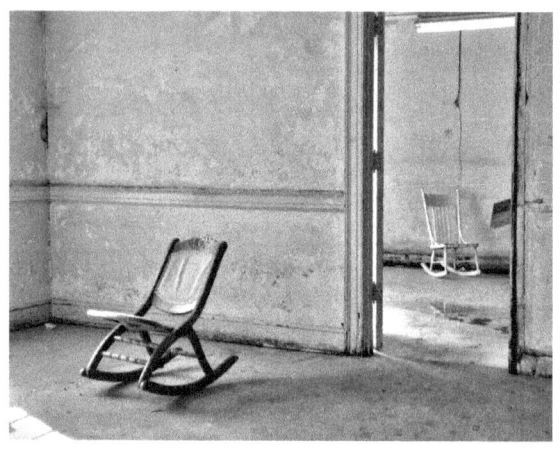

Art Of Life

RELATIONSHIPS

YOU may be talking to a ghost! Stop holding people captive in their past. Let people move on. Yesterday is yesterday. Today is today. So what they f**ked up somehow in their past...YOU will or have as well. One day your going to wish people would let you grow.

You don't have to be a saint to be encouraging...you're not a sell out if you choose to change your life and move in a direction not familiar with your peers...

Displaying hate because of another persons light is shining shows that you don't recognize how much light you have.

Try highlighting and encouraging what is positive in people.... we all were given a few cards we may not have given our self if we could have chose.

Most people cannot read your mind and don't know your story or who you really are. You must express yourself.

Leave clues to your favorite state of mind

Say something uplifting to someone it will make you feel better. Compliment someone else and YOU will feel good cause you made them feel good. YOU get what YOU give.

Even though it hurts don't throw it back at them.

It's not always the case that people don't care about what your dealing with in your life...often they just have their own issues to deal with.

One of the coolest things about new friendships is being exposed to someone else's music collection.

Hold your thoughts until you know all sides to the story...people will always tell the story in a light that is to their best interest.

Keep your light on! Someone may be in a dark tunnel/hole somewhere trying to find his or her way out.

When you begin to dissect the craftsmanship of the people who inspire you.... you will find a person who was inspired by others which leads you to more people to be inspired by.

Shine without knocking others.

Trying to hurt others "intentionally" will only hurt YOU in the long run.

People coming together and supporting each other is how we are able to do things that appear as if they're impossible to accomplish.

Your soul has a family just like your physical body does.

As long as we are in these bodies there will be difficulties seeing things from another person's point of view. We think we can easily but it takes practice and dedication to develop the skill just like everything else. You can see their shoes but you still have yours on.

Careful with the seeds you are planting...you may have to cross back through those thorns

and poisonous fruits if you're planting those
kind of seeds.

It's not mandatory for people to understand
you or agree with you. You must at some
point be willing to charter into the territory
your heart and intuition leads you with or
without allies.

If you see potential in someone be kind and
point it out. They may not realize it yet.

Separation is an illusion. Helping others
succeed is helping you succeed.

We don't have to control everything we are
fascinated by.

Ultimatum lover-a person who will only love
you the way they want. If that demand is not
met they will not love you at all.

It is wise NOT to take vengeance/revenge
upon those who trespass or betray you...you
just end up being just like them...helping to
perpetuate a vicious

never ending cycle.... let

the creator take care of it.... his justice is/will always be greater than ours could ever be.

You can tell a lot about a person by the people that surround them.

Respect that we travel in different lanes.

People be careful. Don't play games with peoples hearts. You never know what type of explosive you're tampering with.

It's really NOT a thin line between love and hate. I feel if you hate someone you once loved then perhaps you never truly loved them in the first place.

Even though it happens and often there is nothing you can do about it. It's still a strange isolating feeling to be misunderstood by someone, especially when you know that their perception is not correct.

Just because your friend(s) has a disagreement or falling out with someone it does not mean that you are obligated to adopt their same feelings about that person. I will never treat a

person different based off of someone else's experiences with them.

Some people have you locked in a prison of your old self in their mind. They have no idea how to relate to the new you. Give/allow people the liberty, right, and respect to change. Stop relating to the old them. When this happens the worst thing we can do is "act" like our former self because it's easy or makes them comfortable. Change/grow and stick to it. Stay on course. Everything is ok we just grow at different rates and that's ok. Sometimes a person may just need a new introduction!

You are not bound to people's perception of you.

Relationships without romance are boring.

Friends who love even the ugly you are the best.

Boyfriends & Girlfriends: When you establish a true friendship first it's like installing a safe

mode or system restore you can always resort to when the romantic relationship experiences turbulence.

You may not be able to do what is done for you for the people who help you but just make sure you do what you can do to let the people who helped you know that you appreciate them.

If you have not done so, tell the people in your life what they mean to you NOW!!!!

Be mindful of how you treat the people in your life. Don't forget who has been there for you.

People like texting because they can take as long as they want to respond.

Everyone is misunderstood by someone.

It feels good to be able to treat your mother to lunch.

Be a blessing to someone.

Tell someone you love that you love them today. Sometimes that's all a person needs to hear or know to help get them through what they are going through.

If somebody isn't feeling you and they feel that you don't fit in their world let them go. Leave them alone. There are about 7 billion people on this planet. Someone else is out there that does want you in his or her world.

Sneak and put $10 in one of your friend's pocket!

Keep yourself in the company of positive encouraging people as much as possible.

The people you love should never have to guess or wonder about your

love for them.

You're blessed if you've found the people that love you.

Your value should NOT be defined by how the last selfish asshole treated you.

I love when I get to communicate on a higher level with someone...all the unspoken stuff...body language, energy, and being aware of each other's subtext.

Cherish your loved ones NOW. Let the people in your life know how much you care often. We never know the hour or who is next to be called home. Love NOW don't wait!

Communication is very important in ALL relationships!

You know you love, are in love, have love etc. for someone when you look or think of them and think about how much you would love to be in their company forever.

Understanding is hard to come by. People see what they want to see.

Buy local. Invest local. Hire local. Promote local. Build local.

You don't really know a person until you see their not so pretty side or when things may not go the way they expect.

Fellas be kind, teach by example, and take good care of your lady so the next guy who dates her can have a great girlfriend!

Encourage every person you cross.

Transitions: I wonder do butterflies miss the caterpillars they use to hangout with.

One of the coolest things about meeting new people is hearing their music collection.

Don't treat him like a man...or treat her like a woman. Just treat them like a human.

There is NO glory or honor in being a cheater...there is NOTHING respectable about it. The idea of side chicks/side dudes is pure bs...there's nothing cool about it.... someone needs to just tell it like it is and free the one playing the fool. (Tables ALWAYS

turn...karma will NOT skip your name when she's making her rounds)

If you have ONE person who gives a sh!t about you in any way then you are blessed!

Nothing beats an encouraging beautiful woman.

Not cool to lock people in the past...people change and grow...let them go.

If you jump in a relationship with someone fresh out of one...chances are you will not be speaking to a whole person yet and chances are your every move will be compared to the last one they were with. Its human to do so.

Be an ear for someone. Society forces us to hold a lot in.

It's better if two people come together as whole people! Not halves or thirds…love and know your self first. Then you can start trying to take on others! You're setting yourself up wrong if you go in looking for missing parts

to yourself…. that's not their responsibility to fill in your blanks!

Sometimes u "may" have to get fcked over many different ways by someone you love to discover if you have the ability to love someone unconditionally!

One of the hardest things is not caring about reciprocity. Being who you are and doing you without it being returned.

If you're not going to love her then just leave her alone so someone else can and she can receive it!!!

I really like getting to know people who appear mean, bitter, or grumpy. They usually end up having a great sense of humor, usually sensitive, and they have lots of character!

It takes great talent to maintain a happy home.

It's cool when there's no grudge or bad blood between the x and the new. Healthy advanced relationships.

Social media is successful because secretly we love each other and we are fascinated with each others lives.

Silence and space can tell you a great deal about the state of your relationship with a person.

Technology brings people together and at the same time it's made it much easier for us to ignore each other.

Just because someone directs evil filled words and energy at you doesn't mean you have to do the same to them.

The world is fascinated with your scars. Most of the time when people pick at them its not that they don't want you to heal they want to

stare at them for a little while so they can
understand their own scars.

There's nothing on Earth like being around
people interested in helping each other be
peaceful and reach higher vibrations.

Its so easy to become cynical and jaded....
positive optimistic people are priceless to me.

Keep yourself around good people who you
care about and who care about you.

People are impacted and look forward to life
when they know someone cares about them.

People are naturally defensive when their core
values and beliefs are challenged. Considering
this while communicating with people opens a
whole new world(s) of understanding.

That feeling you get when you're just happy
you know someone and they know you. When
you're just happy because you're in each
others life.

If people cross your mind you should call and see how they are or go and see them.

The most difficult thing is to respond with light, love, and positive energy when darkness, hate, and negative energy is thrown

at you. You grow with each return blow of positivity.

Never play catch up with people. By the time you get there they will be gone anyway.

Careful what you say to people. You never know where they are in their life.

Keep your self around people who support you and tell you the truth!

Surround yourself around people that care about you and value your existence.

People don't create your emotions...you do...everything is internal but we convince our self otherwise. No one or no thing will always be available to give you the feeling you want to have but you will always be there with you. Get to know yourself. Love yourself. Entertain yourself.

If you are trying to do what you know is right...and the people around you are putting you down for it....you may need to find new

friends that support you when your trying to grow.

Be for others what you wish others would be for you. Be light. Be love. Inspire and encourage others.... (Darkness has no choice but to get out the way when the sun comes up)

You really get to know a person when all their toys are gone.

When people throw hate around often they're really just asking to be loved.

Real friends are more valuable than anything...if you have them...protect each other. Tell them how important they are in your life!

You can really see who someone is.... their true character when they don't get their way.

You don't have to be rich to enrich a kid's life. Spending time does wonders and last much longer. I don't remember all the toys or "stuff" as a kid but I remember the people, the love,

the experiences, and the time they spent with me.

Good friends check up on you and make sure your not forgetting the simple things in life like sleep, eating healthy, fresh air, sunlight, water, visiting family etc.

Share your blessings.

If you surround your self with positive, encouraging, people who vibrate on high frequencies often. It makes it hard to be down long.

Many people just defend the corner they've been backed into.

The company you keep is serious! Observe
the spirit evoked. Be careful not to follow
haters.... heads and bodies are taken as one.

When you shoot venom at someone don't be
surprised when they are slow to take your
offer of something sweet.

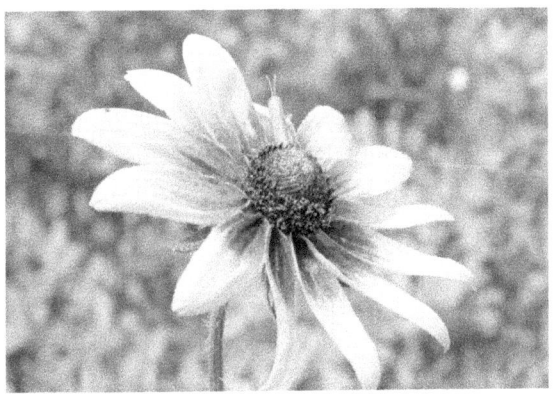

NATURE

Thank goodness the sun isn't selfish or lazy.

Humans are not separate from nature.... its impossible...when we hurt nature we hurt ourselves...when we help we help ourselves.

You're not living until the trees can make you laugh!

Our most advanced technology can't touch nature.

Observe a thing under pressure then you know its true character/makeup.

We must care more for each other. At times it looks like wild animals, insects and plants show more compassion for each other.

What really matter is the water, the air, the land, the plants, the animals, and us. We have to put focus back on what really matters. The use and management of natural resources.

I think there is "a vibration" that is everything and we are parts of it like notes or measures. That's why we have to be mindful of the strings we are pulling on. Everyone impacts someone and they impact others. What you put out there travels much further than we are capable of measuring or perceiving.

Wounded animals will attack you even if you're trying to help them. Humans are no different. Keep this in mind when trying to help all wounded creatures.

I talk to EVERYTHING...myself, plants, animals, the wind, the sun, insects, etc. I'm crazy enough to KNOW they understand me!

Nature is greater than anything we could ever make.

How can the modern world deny the intelligence, the magic, the perfection, and wonder of the natural world....yet we mimic it

in everything we've created. The logic makes
no sense to me. Its like me seeing someone do
something great then I copy what they do and
then knock what I witnessed and copied.

I wonder if light particles talk about how
much darkness is around them....or just be
light.

If we all grow food in our yards and inside our
homes we don't have to worry about food.
GROW FOOD. We have been taught 2 waste
the land we PAY for. It's crucial we break this
cycle! Plants seeds in the yard!

Why should we be granted access to another
life supporting planet when we can't even take
care of the one we have.

Just because the seed you planted has not
poked its head out the ground yet does not
mean its not growing!

NO MATTER what papers they draft up and
sign...there is no justifying...no reasoning to

make it illegal to grow your own food, collect seeds, or share either...it is a birthright!

There's nothing like eating fresh food that you grew from seed!

I feel closest to god out with nature and all the wild and freely growing things. All the stuff we come up with comes from what we observed out there.

NATURE is teaching & reminding us of its power...This world we built is not permanent.

The universe is abundant. Its kind of like a huge cosmic storage room...your thoughts are request...ask and you WILL get it.

One day I'm going to move somewhere where there's absolutely no concrete around...just sunlight, soil, water, trees, air, animals, a little shelter and some love.

The human body was not made by the hands and minds of man nor was the plants and animals we eat to stay alive....we should NOT

be eating food (GMO) made in laboratories...do you trust scientists and corporations who "design" food for the main purpose of profit with your life? As a human race we barely understand how the world works, how the human mind works, the atmosphere, the ocean, weather, how the body works, and how nature works. It is proven fact that genetically modified food causes the human body, and nature harm...they will NOT stop selling it until we stop buying it and demand that we are told what's in the food.

I think the hum heard in silence is the sound of everything at once. Om.

Anybody else ever think the wind is blowing just for you.... like it's trying to communicate with you? (I do)

I like birds.... their songs are very pleasant and peaceful to my ears even though they may only be talking about worms, nest, and bird booty!

Don't be sad when the seed loses its shell. Its purpose has been served. Just keep watering it.

When it gets warm I use to hear and see lots of kids playing in the neighborhoods. Computers and video games are eating all the children. Take the kids to the park. Go camping. Teach them to fish or grow a plant. Visit family. Real human/nature interaction is important.

I talk to myself, animals, plants, the sky, the wind and they all talk back to me.

The universe responds to the effort you put in. If you honestly give something your energy and work for it the rest will start to align.

Nature is the greatest teacher but its on her terms and in her language. You can get the lessons from humans but a lot is lost in translation

Art Of Life

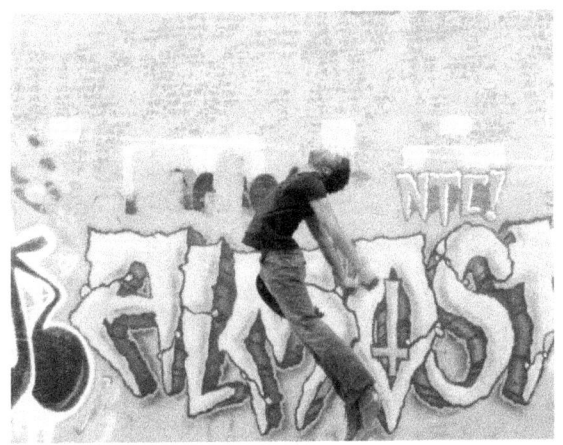

LEARNING

Make the best of all your time...all your moments here on earth. We don't know when we will transition out of here. All the moments are great and have something beneficial to offer you!

Children are little sponges.... or blank computers.... watch what you're teaching them.... they will do what you do a lot quicker than what you say...

You are the sum total of all your experiences.

We should be perpetually excited by the endless possibilities.

Don't let a few bad students make you miss what the teacher is teaching.

Learning to land is just as important as learning to fly.

Reminder: Innovators, trendsetters, & trailblazers. The roads don't ride so smooth before the pavement is down.

Learn to use your super powers. We all have them.

Make your life what you want it to be.

Ignorance is the deadliest weapon of all...hands down...nothing can cause more damage than NOT knowing? Across the board. On ALL levels!

The best distractions are good at convincing you that your energy & attention is needed there.

Don't let the crowd define you....listen to your heart...stick to the mission.

The greatest thing I was ever told was god is within because I use to talk to the sky. Now I talk to myself.

The things that catch your attention are clues to who you are.

There's always something to let go of.

Let us never forget the POWER of ONE.... ONE person can make a HUGE impact in/on life. ONE person can inspire millions of people who can turn and inspire even more. YOU are that 1 person! The simplest approach is starting with our self & how we interact with people & our environment n everyday life at home, at school, at work, during play, the roads, the streets, the halls, online etc. WE ARE NOT SEPARATE WE R CONNECTED!

You can sense where you're wanted and not wanted.

There are no mistakes...everything can teach you something.

Everything is preparing you. The now is preparation for the next. All the steps taken b4 now brought you to the steps you're currently taking. The steps you're currently taking is preparing you for the future steps that you will one day take. Now is always the most crucial moment.

Trust your intuition. It trumps all knowledge learned because god put it there.

Class is everywhere. It's always in session. A perfectly fine-tuned course for you to become your greatest self.

It's so funny how u can listen to a song and not really HEAR it until you experience it for your self. The lyrics come to life!

I have years of information in my head that I must now unlearn!

Growing is not always an enjoyable experience but in the long run it is the greatest feeling one can have.

If I am too sensitive I will be easily scarred (or destroyed) but if I am too cold I will miss the experience(s) of what it is to be alive. This is why balance is important.

Refine your weakness. Don't run from it. Go at it head on until it becomes a new strength.

We must learn to buy from companies that treat workers, animals, and the environment with respect.

The intellectuals/thinkers that the educated world looks to did not have degrees that gave them permission to think...god and nature which are one spoke directly to them and the same is still possible today.

I really love to see people grow.

You don't know you've grown and changed until something are someone invites you to be or act like your old self and you decline the invitation.

Americans get such a fever for battling injustice in other countries but not HERE in our own homes, backyards, neighborhoods,

schools, medical industry, food industry, banking, bogus government policy, the prison industry, and un reliable journalism. Where is that fever?

The real fun starts when you learn that you have no enemies on earth.... you in fact have none but your self...fearing humans is permission to control you.

Experience is the best teacher.

Many things have been made taboo just to keep it from you.

Real woman shouldn't attempt to compete with photoshop skills, perfect even toned skin, no blemishes, no scars, no acne, perfect hair not a stray strand, eyes bleach white, teeth chalk white, bodies re-sculpted and reshaped etc.

Let go of yesterday or you may never see the future...the past can hold you down if you hold on to it.... you may miss your flight into the future!

Always be thankful, hopeful, and encouraged. Theres nowhere to go but up...when you're at the bottom!!!! So when your flying high be happy and THANKFUL when your on the ground...everyone must get low to get high...trying jumping while standing straight up!!!

I am no longer focused or interested in resolving or fighting the darkness rampant in the world or other people. I must focus and resolve the disharmony with in myself b4 I can even think about the world.

Embrace the struggle. It's the only way to get through it. At this point in my life I'm digesting this. If life is hard the only thing you can do about it is work hard to do something about it.

Your strength is in your story. It serves you no good to compare, compete, or envy others. Your journey is unique and specifically for you. Pay attention to everything you have been through. The jewels, swords, and shields are there.

Hey YOU get over it. Its good to say that in the mirror sometimes.

Don't confuse reflections with the source of the light.

Time is not the same in outer space...its just measurement from our perspective...its really just one long day!

I am no longer afraid of what I'm capable of.

Don't be afraid to ask for help and don't be afraid to help.

Please should not call children dumb and stupid...your planting a very bad seed in their brain.

It takes practice being positive and being negative.

Did anyone else think the moon was following you when you were little?

Sometimes you have to go through nasty, unpleasant, dangerous situations to pull out something beautiful.

Grow but never forget the path you've taken.

No matter how much you learn or how far you go remain teachable.

With the right/healthy perspective letting go can be just as beautiful and fulfilling as holding on.

Limit the energy that you feed to your phantom hater. Save it for the real people that love you!

No one is accountable or responsible for your happiness but YOU....get to it!

The universe is always giving us hints.

Pay close attention to what you say and think about yourself...don't accept how the world has defined you, your race, your gender, class, your community etc. We are not done breaking down walls.

The problems in this world are much deeper than 99% vs. 1%, rich vs. poor, person vs. corporate, us vs. them etc. I think the whole planet is having an identity crisis.

Someone taught us to be afraid of our abilities. Someone taught us to hate each other. Someone taught us not to question. Someone taught us to come up with all these excuses and reasons to not even try. We must unlearn these ideas.

I always get in trouble when I start looking on the outside for what is within.

The package is not the contents.

Slaves were never set free they just expanded the plantation.

Don't wait until you have things taken away from you to be thankful for what you have.

Follow your intuition. It's your personal map quest, teacher, compass, director, counselor, etc. It will get you where you're supposed to be!

I'm a voracious reader...I'm completely obsessed with learning. It's like my head has no bottom. No matter how much I learn it still feels empty!

Ladies it is highly attractive to be smart AND beautiful.... mind over body.... there's nothing more magical on earth.

Thank god we have the ability to reprogram our minds.

Don't expect anyone to understand or agree with YOUR path. It is YOUR journey not theirs.

Know yourself. Study yourself. Refine self. Work on self and you will not have time to be caught in the drama of other people's life.

YOU were created specifically to be you. Now dig that!

I don't ever want to stop learning.

This should not be public discourse. For any one to even consider or discuss legitimizing the act of rape is complete mind f*ck*ry. This is an erroneous conversation. It is a blatant display that these people have no idea what is to be human and have compassion for another human being. They are the savages. They are savages in suits parading as learned civilized human beings. Any person who has the mind to justify such a heinous and barbaric act should be barred from practicing any lawmaking and undergo some type of therapy. There is no time or situation that rape is right.

Everything takes PRACTICE.... musician, writer, actor, dancer, being negative, being positive, communication, meditation, having faith etc....even being in a mind state where you want to practice takes practice!

Sometimes you have to switch gears and back up or zoom out to see a situation objectively to make a balanced decision.

Art Of Life

You have to touch the ground to reach the sky.

Whatever you're going through know that god made you strong enough to get through it.

I need to start writing down the moments I feel super inspired & in love with life...maybe there is some kind of pattern.

It doesn't really matter what anyone thinks of you. What really matters is what you think of you because that's what you act on anyway.

When learning to fly you must learn to land.

People are afraid and run from what they asked for when they get it. I see it over and over again in myself and others. Intelligent people make convincing clever excuses perfectly crafted to keep them from what they asked for. Life is short...don't do this.

There's a large amount of people doing great work and no one knows their name.

A.S.H.A. stands for Attention Surplus Hyperactivity Ability...being able to focus on many things in hyper speed.

The illusion of scarcity is what makes money.

I think the pyramids of Giza are amazing forms of ancient technology far superior than our modern gadgets. Think about how much we have learned just from investigating their existence. We learn and grow from them so its like they're transmitting information from the universe to us like antennas!

Don't get stuck on 1 or 2 attributes. Nothing is wrong with it but we are much more capable than just being beautiful, pretty, or sexy. Don't forget that you have the ability of being intelligent, wise, grounded, innovative, a problem solver, imaginative, ambitious, clever, caring, kind, compassionate, loving, fair, humble, and more. I hope this is being passed on in the homes of the young girls and guys growing up. TV radio and print surely is not going to teach it to them.

Just being who and what YOU ARE can be very powerful by itself.

Learn to have self-control or the world will control you. Learn to control yourself or others will.

There is a time to tread lightly and a time to step sure with all your weight. Your intuition will let you know when to do which.

Crazy how what we look for is always somewhere close to us.

Even in sadness there's still a few drops of joy.

This world is flooded with suggestions, demands, commands, laws, mandates, amendments, philosophies, theories, trends, memes, advertisements and subliminal messages telling you who you should be and what you should do with your life. Everyone can give an opinion but that's all they are. The greatest thing you can do is follow YOUR HEART and listen to YOUR INTUITION.

Just be yourself and what is meant for you will present and make itself available to you.

Don't chase money...chase what makes you valuable....nurture your talent/skill(s) then $ will knock on your door or call your phone because you have something to offer/contribute.

There are some things we must learn that we don't want to know but we must in order to grow.

You are not a slave to consumer culture. You love yourself and your neighbors. You are beautiful. You believe the possibilities are endless. Your potential for greatness is boundless. You have hope for humanity. You are a problem solver. You are not selfish. You are sensitive to the human suffering experienced on this planet. You have good taste in music. You support local entrepreneurs and artists. You don't run red lights. There is no such thing as legitimate rape. You want to adopt a kid one day. You want to reduce your carbon footprint. You are concerned about the future that the children will be given. You love learning and growing.

You are not racist. You engage in the activities in your community. You recycle. You care about the environment. You respect the different views of others. You donate to

local charities. You donate blood from time to time. You believe in natural healing. You have the drive to be a great human everyday. You have a sense of humor. You agree that love is better than war. You don't watch reality TV shows. You love reading books. You know how to agree to disagree.

Push yourself beyond your limits. That's how you really grow.

Everyday is a chance to do something you've always wanted to do.

Positivity. Pass it on.

The limitations you see are in your mind...the universe has no limits.

We have a great deal of lies to unlearn.

Don't chase money master what makes you valuable.

Time is precious. Go for it now. Give it ALL you got!!! If you don't give it your ALL its NOT worth doing. If you give it YOUR ALL it doesn't matter what anyone else thinks about it.

Don't be afraid to jump off the track that you and your peers are on if you come to a point where your feet tell you to go a different direction.

Whatever it is. Get over over it and be present.

Songs become a part of you after you listen to them. Kind of like the artist grafted their thoughts onto yours or exposed you to another spectrum of emotion.

Never be afraid of making a fool of yourself...you might miss out on bringing someone great joy!

We find our greatest strengths and gifts during our darkest moments in life. These times we struggle the most is when we discover our

virtues. Don't avoid the test. The results are fruits that YOU grew for your benefit.

The fear of something will often do more damage than the thing you fear actually happening.

One of the most valuable things taught to me as a kid was to not be afraid to ask questions.... if you don't know, ask. If people don't have the answers...ask the creator and the answer will bloom within!

Situations/experiences only bring out what's already in you.

Why should aliens show their self to us...look at how bad we treat those that are different who we can see.

Be thankful and have faith when you have nothing and soon that will change. Be grateful for the small things then more will come.

We can't give up on the good fight. We cant stop loving and shining our light. We must

keep seeking the truth. Every little bit counts. A little evil can go a long way...so can a little good. You are significant not because you're better than anyone else but simply because you're here.

Do something each day that will bring you closer to your dreams becoming reality.

Wallets and pocketbooks move the markets even more than your votes do. Buying and selling is the real campaign. Where you spend your money is a louder statement than all the words you speak. That's why people can take to the streets with signs and yell for months and nothing changes. Just remember where you spend your money is liken to a vote.

Be mindful of your contribution. It only takes a small amount to tip someone or a situation either way.

Everyday we add something new to our autobiography. Make it interesting!

My Top Things To Witness While Visiting Earth List. (What's yours?) 1. Birth of a human or any living creature. 2. A plant or animal growing when the odds are against it. 3. To see thoughts manifested in the physical realm. 4. The harmony in chaos. 5. How it feels to truly love someone. 6. How it feels to be truly loved. 7. The creator working through you to bless others. 8. The creator working through others to bless you. 9. The spirit and CHARACTER of nature. 10. The blatant denial of facts and evidence. 11. To see death/transition. 12. When the under dog wins!

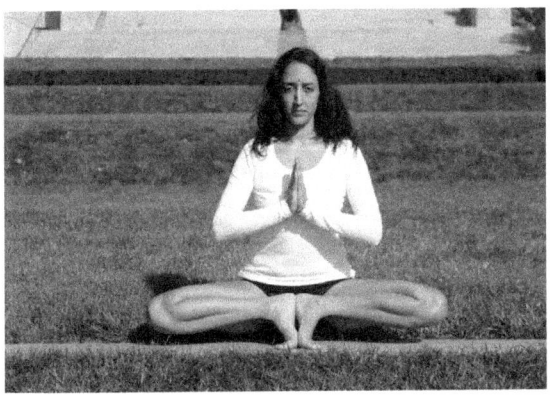

MIND BODY & SOUL

Thoughts and emotions have volume knobs.

Grow food metaphorical and literally!

Attitude has a smell.

Even in storms there is a place inside you that will remain still.

You are the architect of your self-image.

Be present. Stay in the now. Too far ahead or in the past is where it gets complicated.

Rub your "lamp" there's a genie in us!
#Genius

There is something that only you were put here to do and you can find it by paying attention to what resonates with you.

The Earth turns 1 degree every 4 minutes, which is the same as our heartbeat to breath ratio -- 4 pulse beats per breath. We are all connected.

It is physically and spiritually impossible for you to ever be alone. Tap into that!

All the parts of my body are happier when I use them.

Your body has trillions of cells. They are all receiving and transmitting. Your body is listening and speaking!

I am my own personal servant. This guy Damon will do whatever I tell him to do. If I teach him correctly, feed him, love him, inspire him, nourish his abilities, and discipline him....There is no end to the possibilities of what we may accomplish together.

The human spirit is great beyond our comprehension. We are walking talking compact universes with the ingredients of all that is within us. We can overcome it all if we REALLY CHOOSE   TO!

If u strike a tuning fork near a tuning fork that is tuned to the same note of the one u just tapped the other will begin to vibrate because they resonate on the same frequency....humans are no different.

Self-analysis is key to growth. Get out of the habit of blaming others and making excuses. You are an instrument and just like a musical instrument you must be tuned and adjusted so you can hit the right notes.

If you were told that your words could kill or give life.... would you try to learn and choose your words carefully?

Perception really is everything and it takes practice to keep a healthy one.

No matter how far we grow in age the child is always present.

Malnutrition is another way to become depressed.

God is in you. He used his self to create you.

You don't need drugs to get high. Your mind is more powerful than we have been taught.

Your face keeps the emotions you feel the most.

Don't be afraid to redefine yourself.

The money making machine wants you to believe that your natural beauty is not good just the way it is but that's far from the truth. The creator of the universe made you and your beautiful as you are. Remember that!

The greatest wars/battles are waged lost and won in the mind.... the physical actions we take are a result of what went down in the mind

What's in your heart and mind dictates what your footsteps and hands will do.

Every thought and mood has a frequency.... each state even has weight....the higher ones are always lighter.

Keep an open mind. The universe will always be much larger than the space your head fills. Empty that cup and fill with something fresh!

At any point and time YOU can access the GREATNESS that is within YOU.

LOVE IS an adaptogen. An adaptogen is a metabolic regulator which increases the ability of an organism to adapt to environmental factors, and to avoid damage from such factors. Love does that for us.

You would be surprised at the magical healing powers of simple things like water, sunlight, fresh air, laughter, and rest can do.

You can get high without drugs.

The myth and magic of vagina: Its self cleansing, self healing, self lubricating, its internal and external at the same time, there's millions of people at any given moment seeking its attention, there's entire industries dedicated to it, stories are written about it, songs are made about it, poetry is written about it, museums around the world are full of paintings of it, people go crazy for it, it has hundreds of nicknames, some people are afraid of it, some men (and women) are held captive and controlled by it, its able to cause extreme pleasure and give pleasure in any setting any time of year, a whole NEW HUMAN BEING grows there! Now that's pretty darn mythical and magical to me!

I'm pregnant with my new self and I'm dying to meet him.

Be good to yourself...this relationship will outlast all others.

Some people don't believe it but the type of music/entertainment a person listens to and watches has a lot to do with their state of mind.

The human body has about 100 trillion cells. Each cell transmits and receives data like a small antenna. So be mindful of what you think. Trillions are listening!

Every drop of energy spent counts. Move wisely.

I'm thankful for my life. I'm thankful for the path I'm on.

Be conscious of what you will into reality. What you think and say is more powerful than what we have been led to believe.

Everyone should nap or sleep outside every once in a while.

Treat your brain like your stomach and fill it with good healthy information.

Provoke thought: How much of how you live your life is actually your idea? We are robbed of our time to think. We are bombarded with other peoples thoughts non stop 360 degrees. Is independent thinking becoming a lost activity? Functioning within the walls of society...when is there anytime to think freely for ones self. I mean time to think your thoughts and no one elses. Have you done that lately? Are you sure they were yours and not someone elses? Is it in the am while preparing for work? Is it in traffic on the way to work? Is it on lunch break before one heads back to work? Is it in traffic on the way home from work? Is it while preparing dinner? Is it while reading? Is it while watching tv? While listening to music? While cleaning? While working out? While in the shower? While preparing for bed? While making love? While dreaming? Whens the last time you had time to stop and think??? Is there ever time to think and only think while not doing anything else? Do you agree or disagree because you thought about it or because you sided with a group? Do you think of solutions to the problems this world faces? Do you ever think about whats outside the multiple choice boxes and circles? Make time to think.....

You're more attractive when you're just doing your thing...don't try so hard...god already made you beautiful.

Eating real fresh fruits and veggies is better than supplements.

Treat your mind like a house.... make it a place you like to be in.

If nothing more celebrate because you exist.

We are not skin color. We are not bank accounts. We are not credit cards. We are not our possessions. We are not our religions. We are not our social class. We are not our physical locations. We occupy them but we are not our physical bodies.

I am...I am the captain of my spaceship...I am the ship...I am the space.... I am the ruler and the time...I am the curve. I am the line...I am the searched I am the find.

Don't ever think for a moment that you don't have power. You are lying to yourself or someone else is lying to you if you believe that you don't. Use it for something good. It DOES make a difference.

Treat your self as if you were pregnant with your future self because you are. Good day friends and family!

Why didn't god give us ear lids?

Embrace what makes you unique. Nurture that.

It's funny how most of the time it seems a person must die/leave their flesh for people to see who they were...what they were doing with their life. Maybe cause the flesh is no longer in the way? It would be great if we could truly appreciate/see people while they are alive.

The heart has a mind of its own.

The brain needs time to digest just like the stomach does.

Life is too short not to make the most of it.

The body is just a spacesuit that allows your spirit to live in this world.

In warfare the first attacks are on the mind. This type of attack is continuous and unannounced. Protect your mind. Guard your thoughts.

Light your way with the light within.

Your face isn't the only part of your body that smiles.

Don't worry about falling. Your wings will appear when you need them.

Nurturing your ability to self motivate and inspire yourself is one of the best things you can do.

Sometimes we have to get broken all the way down just to be in the mind state to ask, "Show me the way. Show me what I am suppose to do."

Be the vision of you that you see in your minds eye. That is the true you.

Theory: What if so-called mental illnesses add, adhd, borderline personality disorder, schizophrenia, bipolar etc were really just untapped/untrained natural human abilities/powers/resources. The Earth has two north and south poles __ so should we right?

Perhaps those "dis orders" are pathways to that big % of the brain we don't use.

Love your self...learn to enjoy your own company...get to know your self...take a walk...take a ride...take your self out...no one is to blame for your unhappiness or boredom...life is big and vast...there's no excuse...explore self if that's all u got!

Everyone should have some peaceful place to go to gather or release thoughts. Some place to get grounded when you need.

Your gut feeling is your engine.

Your life is the script. You are the writer & the actor. Everywhere all the time is the stage, the TV, and the movie screen. You are the witness and the thing witnessed.

Your body is music the universe made.

We all have magical powers.

I think people who are not afraid to lose their vessel/life have been given a glimpse of eternal life.

Life is full of infinite possibilities. The limits are set by your thoughts.

Attention deficit hyperactivity disorder also known as a.d.h.d. NO! More like attention surplus hyperactivity ability a.s.h.a.!

There's never a need for jealousy and envy. You have the ability to produce any light you see.

You're not the only one thinking what you're thinking! Space is not the only thing we share

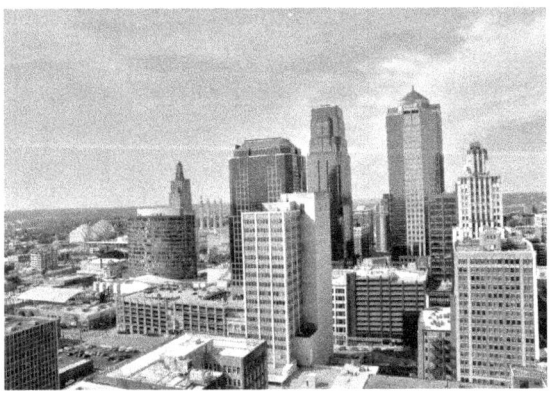

THE HUMAN CONDITION

As long as we continue to agree with this reality...this is what it will be.

We, our, and us is always better and more powerful than I, me, and my!

The greatest moments are when I totally forget how old I am, what color my skin is, what gender I am, what country I live in, what city, and what class I fit in. That's when I really feel alive.

If we treated our self and others like everyday was our birthday the world would be transformed overnight.

We have to stop chasing after money. Money is an illusion created to control the masses minds and the real resources.

You are not a man or a woman. You are not a white man or a white woman. You are not a black man or a black woman. You are not a democrat, a liberal or   a republican. You are not a baptist, catholic, muslim, or an atheist. You are not any of these labels. You are a human being. We are something else all together and all this mess is to keep you from discovering what that is.

Don't underestimate the power of 1! One person can cause a great ripple effect that can be felt by the whole world. You matter!

When the gate opens many creatures will choose to stay in the cage.

I think when humans stop fighting.... we will be able to access our FULL potential.

Creating/giving birth is one of the most beautiful profound happenings we as human beings take part in.

It is what it is UNTIL we make it something else.

Society is like a family and the government is like that societies parents. It's no wonder the people think, behave, and resolve conflicts they way they do.

The best way to find life on other planets is to take care of this one. I mean what intelligent life form in their right mind would send invitations and coordinates to us in our current collective state.

The people in power (the ones hidden not the puppets) know that all humans have super powers and are capable of unlimited and unimaginable abilities...the structure of society/the establishment and all we see is designed to keep us from all that we are truly capable of. This is done by limiting information, poisoning us through food/fluids, air quality, entertainment, dividing us through war, mental distractions, etc. If we were to operate at our full capacity there would be no purpose for those in power.

Imagine what we can do together.

People at war over physical locations.... it's never been about that.... the places talked about in ancient text are just symbols/symbolic representation for spiritual principles! Vessels/buildings/land/matter.

The creator put us in what could perhaps be the most beautiful environment in the universe for all we know equipped with everything we could possibly ever need...yet we are to busy fighting each other to enjoy it.

All the movements lose momentum because we keep forgetting & losing sight that we are all human before any other label.

Don't get caught up in a cycle...just cause mommy, daddy, sister, brother, your neighborhood, cousins, friends, your city, your country, or whoever is in that cycle doesn't mean you have to continue it.

Even we are NOT aware we are still a part of something much greater than our self!

Today exercise your power to make life better. You never know how far it will echo into the future.

Let your greatness free. We need you.

Each generation two torches are handed down. One side bent on destruction, lies, and manipulation of the masses. One side sent to build, heal, create, and continue to manifest peace and love.

You're a star in someone's dark sky. Don't hide your light.

God splits up information like a torrent file so we have to work together to see the whole picture.

One of the greatest things I would love to see happen on earth is all the worlds governments agreeing and coming together to do something serious about the condition of the worlds water and soil. We as a species should elevate to a position as caretakers of our one planet. We should be ashamed and concerned as a species that we cannot drink water from our rivers, creeks, and lakes, yet we have the audacity to be looking for other planets that are in a condition to sustain life.

We are walking books. We are walking televisions. We are newspapers. We are speakers. Reality is what we are all making it at every moment and every thought. So inspire someone somewhere sometime!

Personal issues are global issues.

Life is perfect & BEAUTIFUL if we have the eyes and heart to see it that way.

I pray all the broken, jaded, and hurting hearts will be healed, renewed, and refreshed.

There's never really a time that our actions and words don't impact others in some way.

I really miss the honesty from childhood. Kids say exactly what they think and feel. Adults have way too many layers. Decoding behavior all the time can be draining.

If you see me in public, remind me to talk about super powers.

If you see a positive man or women...know that it's not an easy stride to BE that...they are at war even if YOU can't see it. Thank them for overcoming. Thank them for their strength. We can ALL pull from each other's strength, love, and beauty. Lets stop reinventing the wheel and join forces.

If MLK.... one person can cause this much change.... imagine what we can ALL do with our lives.... How can we best serve humanity? How can we use our gifts to improve life?

If you are bound to people only of your race/ethnicity you have not even began to live life yet.

I think Asian cultures are super awesome. I really admire their connection with the earth, fashion, their preventative approach to medicine, their teaching methods, fashion, literature, their appreciation of beauty, the way they preserve their history etc. The rest of the world can learn a lot from them.

We should all speak in public more. If nothing more just to acknowledge each other's presence. It's not that difficult to at least nod, say hello, good morning, or good evening.

I think my greatest strength is I remain happy to be amongst the living. I have a perpetual fascination with life.

We are all connected even if we can't see the connections. They are there.

Don't underestimate the power of a smile.... particularly YOUR smile!

White people, brown people, yellow people, and black people is false. People are not colors!

How felons are treated by society after they have served time needs to be revisited.

We must make our learning facilities a top priority.

When I was younger I had no clue what it really meant...but as I grew/grow I began to see the power that love has...love REALLY could/can change the world. The biggest impact we can make is with those around us. Family, friends, neighbors, strangers in passing, coworkers, etc....love more!

If you have kids in your life encourage them, expose them to lots of different stuff outside of TV and video games.... most importantly

SUPPORT their dreams! You never know how much it will help them in life.

Everything in this world is related and closely connected. Nothing in this world is separate AT ALL! The sooner we begin to truly meditate and digest this concept the sooner we can all elevate to the level of our greatest manifestation. Beware of the vibes you let in, how you respond to them, and what you put out. Recognize the off notes and find the resolve. We are notes.... WE ARE THE MUSIC!

Don't you see?????.... People we have to come together.... Stop fighting.... stop trying to get over.... STOP HATING ONE ANOTHER.... Just enjoy what YOU have and congratulate another's success. Theres other ways to solve things other than primal brute violence.

Two questions citizens must at some point start asking: 1. Does my job hurt or oppress someone? 2. Do I spend my money with businesses that support or help my community?

Will the human race ever agree that war is a useless outdated method for solving problems?

The greatest changes must take place in us! Many laws and policies are in need of change but the ones we live by everyday are really the ones that need changing. If YOU cant see a SHIFT coming/happening you are not paying attention. 1 by one we make up the whole. We are the people who lived in this era. Just remember how each of us treat ourselves and each other make up what is happening in the whole world. There is power in one. I have power in my everyday decisions and choices. YOU have power in your everyday decisions and choices. We each have a part to play...........we cant make the world better until we first make our self better...we cant make the world better until we make our families better...we cant make the world better until we make our neighborhoods better.

Sometime when you "reach back" and help someone who may not be as far as you...that person ends up being the one who helps you through when you need help. When you can always help others. Don't be afraid that you will lose your spot or light. There is plenty for everyone!

They designed this society for slaves. Point blank. Everything else is propaganda to keep the illusions intact. Look or act anything like Morpheus then prepare for adversity.

We need to recreate what has been stolen and hidden from us...which is how to be a human family sharing the same planet and resources. (AGAIN)

Communities need to be self-sustainable. Everything in walking distance. The indigenous cultures had/have it right. The village setting is the best model. Being locked away isolated in our little worlds is unhealthy and hurts society as a whole.

Encourage the children around you. Encourage your friends to do their best.

Share your gifts, skills, and abilities when you can.

Truthfully people in powerful elite positions in the world are not the ones who will change the world. Its everyday people like YOU and I.

Humans should lose their right to see colors until we all learn to get along.

Super heroes are real!

Racism stems from ignorance. Once you know certain things about our existence you have no choice but to see there is no reason to be racist. We come from the same source!

The world needs more problem solvers.

We only have to see one of us do what is believed to be impossible once. Then the rest of us will know it is possible and believe we can go even farther than that.

There is sooo much happening around the world that is not being shown in major media outlets. Major corporations, banks, and other hidden entities are attempting to control what

information is being put out. It's not in their interest to share good info with us because of the money and face they stand to lose. Good meaning info that teaches us to heal, learn, advance, grow, break free, live natural, live healthy, live with less, raise healthy children, cut cost on food, cut cost on utility bills etc. So it's up to US to stop ALLOWING ourselves to be distracted. We must fully take advantage of these tools and our ability to connect with one another and change our conditions. We must NOT forget that WE power the system with our lives and our loyalty. We must understand that when we spend money we are voting. We must understand that where we work matters. Work for a company that has a good cause. Spend money local!

There is something very attractive about people who attempt what seems impossible. Perhaps they remind us of what is possible.

If WE stop buying all the toxic crap in the stores.... (Spoiled, processed, gmos etc).... they must either go bankrupt or sell better products!!!!! If we keep buying they will keep selling it.........supply/demand.

Our lives are letters to the future.

We are on The USS Enterprise (NCC-1701).... Earth is a starship! We are moving through space on or inside this thing and we have passengers so this is totally some type of ancient cosmic super spaceship!

I am Cherokee, Choctaw, Jamaican, Blackfoot, Irish, German, Ethiopian, Jewish, and Spanish as far as I know as of now. It would be a form of self-deprecation and disrespect to myself and everyone that came before me if I chose only to recognize one dynamic "African American" I have no choice but to have love for all people. WE ARE ALL PEOPLE!

We are ALL being elevated...even if we didn't ask for it.

We have to start identifying ourselves as human beings and not colors. We have to see ourselves as spiritual beings in physical bodies. We are   energy in capsules.

The reason a small amount of people can rule the world is because it's easier for them to come to an agreement.

Circumstances don't matter only state of being matters! Matter is created by state of being! Get out there and create better circumstances!

Don't be afraid to let your light shine. We all need each other!

The message is clear. Is it not? Governments and big corporations are cutting everything that really matters to people and their well being but are increasing support for things that are harmFULL to human life. These are crimes against humanity. We must do much ourselves!

Share what you know because it may be just the info we are missing.

I always think about WHAT it was that Martin Luther King Jr. saw that allowed him to continue his mission even in the face of

ridicule, danger, and death...I hope WE ALL
get to see what he did one day.

Imagine the conflict of the people who are
mixed. How do you side with half or
percentages of yourself? You cant and you
shouldn't try to or be asked to.

Truthfully anyone who voted because of race
has been fooled by the theatrics of American
politics.

People are people in every race. All tempted
by the same forces.

Greed is causing the imbalance. We as a
species have the ability to make sure every
living person on earth has clean water, good
food, and shelter. It's a known fact that we
have the capabilities to make this happen but
we must move beyond fear of scarcity to do
so.

Listen. We are all connected. There is no separation between us. You are not your skin color. You are not your class. You are not

your bank account or credit score. You are something more. WE are something more. We are one and we must treat and behave as one or else this cycle will continue to repeat itself.

Non celebrities seek what celebrities have and experience....celebrities seek normalcy and peace.

Human thought and emotion is studied, known, and used to hit you where it will be effective. The goal is simple: Make you the consumer feel like your life is missing something. It's not complete until you have this or that product.

As long as there's a buyer there will be sellers.

Out in space searching for life and all we keep finding is mirrors.

Less seeking more realizing and acknowledging what already is.

The greatest method for "keeping" slaves is to hide the fact that they are slaves.... ignorance is only bliss to those who profit from it!

The best thing the leaders of a country can do is provide people with the highest quality education, arts programs, and healthcare possible for FREE.... creative healthy intelligent people CREATE jobs